RHODE ISLAND

Unforgettable Vintage Images of the Ocean State

Note from the Publisher

Royalties from the sale of this book will be paid into a fund for historic preservation to be administered by Arcadia Publishing. We envisage that proceeds from the fund will go toward supporting local history projects in the community. For further details, please contact us at Arcadia's Midwest office.

RHODE ISLAND

Unforgettable Vintage Images of the Ocean State

ARCADIA

First published 2000.

Published by:
Arcadia Publishing, Inc.
3047 N. Lincoln Ave., Suite 401
Chicago, IL 60657

Typesetting and origination by Tempus Publishing, Inc.
Printed and bound in Great Britain.

Library of Congress Number: 00-105699
ISBN 0-7385-0755-5

For all general information contact Arcadia Publishing at:
Telephone 843-853-2070
Fax 843-853-0044
E-Mail sales@arcadiapublishing.com

For customer service and orders:
Toll-Free 1-888-313-2665

Visit us on the internet at http://www.arcadiapublishing.com

Contents

ACKNOWLEDGMENTS

Arcadia would like to thank these authors for their contributions to this volume:

George Adams	*East Providence*
Robert Bellerose	*Woonsocket*
John Chaney	*Warren*
Betty Cotter	*Kingston* *Peace Dale* *South Shore* *Wakefield*
Don D'Amato	*Block Island* *Pawtuxet* *Warwick*
Nancy Devin	*Portsmouth* *Tiverton and Little Compton Volume II*
Kathleen Fink	*Westerly*
Joe Fuoco	*Federal Hill* *Knightsville and Silver Lake* *Rhode Island's Mill Villages*
Tom and Barbara Greene	*North Providence*
Eleanor Guy	*Scituate*
Elizabeth Johnson	*Pawtucket*
Edna Whitaker Kent	*Gloucester*
Salli Latimer	*Narragansett*

Sarah Leavitt	*Slater Mill*
Rob Lewis	*Newport*
Ruth Marris Macauley	*Warren*
Louis McGowan	*Johnston*
Patricia Mehrtens	*Burrillville*
Sean Paul Milligan	*Quonset Point Naval Air Station* *Quonset Point Naval Air Station Volume II*
Scott Molloy	*All Aboard: The History of Mass Transit in Rhode Island*
Joe Muratore	*Italian Americans in Rhode Island*
Lydia L. Rapoza	*Cranston*
Susan Reed	*Pawtucket*
Charles Savoie	*The Lower Blackstone River Valley*
Walter Schroeder	*Davisville and the Seabees* *Dutch Island and Fort Greble*
Richard V. Simpson	*America's Cup: The Rhode Island Connection* *Bristol* *Tiverton and Little Compton Volume II*
Brigid Rooney Smith	*Watch Hill*
James Wheaton IV	*University of Rhode Island*
Lionel Wyld	*The Navy in Newport*

Introduction

Rhode Island may be the smallest state in the Union, but it does have the longest official name: "The State of Rhode Island and Providence Plantations." At about 1,045 square miles, you could fit nearly 500 Rhode Islands into the state of Alaska. But because of Narragansett Bay slicing into its eastern side, Rhode Island boasts 384 miles of shoreline, and 36 offshore islands.

Archaeologists have found evidence of life in this part of New England dating back more than 8,000 years. When the first European travelers arrived, they found a substantial population of Native Americans, including the largest of these nations, the Narragansett. This group was a part of the larger Algonquin family of nations which stretched from southern Canada to North Carolina. Along with the Narragansett were the Wampanogs, the Nipmucks, the Cowesetts, the Shawomets, and the Niantics.

It was in 1636 that the first permanent settlement of Europeans was established by Roger Williams and his followers. They came seeking freedom of worship, something they could not find in the repressive atmosphere of the nearby Massachusetts Bay Colony. The establishment of Providence Plantations (which, as noted above, is still part of the official state name) opened the door to many more religious groups to enter Rhode Island and take advantage of the religious tolerance practiced there. The first Baptist sect in America was established here in 1639, the first Quakers came in 1677, and Rhode Island became home to many Jews in the 17th and 18th centuries. In fact, Touro Synagogue in Newport is believed to be the oldest synagogue in the country, being established in 1736.

Although the smallest of the original 13 colonies, Rhode Island was by no means the quietest. In a bold move, the General Assembly of the Colony of Rhode Island declared independence from Great Britain on May 4, 1776—two full months before the rest of the 12 colonies. And the citizens of Providence destroyed British tea before the more famous Tea Party in Boston.

Today, Rhode Island is home to much more civilized competition such as the America's Cup Race, and it houses the Tennis Hall of Fame. From the mansions of Newport and the Cliff Walk and the skyscrapers of Providence, from the mill towns and river valleys, from Block Island to Woonsocket, nearly a million people call Rhode Island home. We have gathered the best images from the Rhode Island collection *Images of America* series books into this volume. We hope you will cherish these unforgettable images of the people and places of this Ocean State.

Tom Rakness
Editor, Arcadia Publishing

One

People

Knightsville is known to some residents as Monkeytown, and Cranston Street leading to Knightsville is sometimes referred to as Monkeytown Road. One legend has it that a local lad joined a seafaring voyage, and when he returned he brought back a most unusual creature with him—a monkey in a cage. People traveled from all over to see the animal. Monkeytown is hardly a respectable name for the community named after the Knight family, who owned much of the land and was dominant in state and local government.

All children in the area remember the metal Whitcomb dog located in the Whitcomb Farm front yard in East Providence.

The popular and talented Fire King Fife and Drum Corps Band was in demand throughout Rhode Island. The group enhanced just about any celebration and was a source of pride to the village. This photograph was taken in front of Harmony Lodge next to Trinity Church c. 1930. (Henry A.L. Brown Collection.)

History was made in September 1957, when Marine Helicopter Squadron One (HMX-1) performed the first Presidential lift with the original Marine One helicopter, a Sikorsky HUS-1Z. Dwight David Eisenhower flew from the Summer White House in Newport to Quonset when he was required to return to Washington on short notice. (*Quincy Point Naval Air Station* by Sean Paul Michigan.)

The village of Pawtuxet, with its bridge, falls, and charm, has always attracted artists. In 1939, these artists tried to capture the scene from the lower level of the bridge adjacent to Bishop's Garage, which is now Hunter's Garage. (William Hall Library Collection.)

Peace Dale's Citizens' Band is shown here in a photograph thought to have been taken around 1904. Frequently booked at the Wakefield Opera House, the band was popular throughout town and played an important role in the age before movies and television. W. Frank Holland was the director, and Paul W. Dixon was the manager. The Citizens' Band was probably the first act to play on the Village Green. On July 31, 1908, the *Narragansett Times* reported that the band "gave a very pleasing open air concert" on that Tuesday evening. In September 1894, the then-"Citizens' Cornet Band" of Peace Dale serenaded T.A. Gardner's home on Main Street in Wakefield on a Saturday evening, according to the *Times*. (Courtesy of Pettaquamscutt Historical Society.)

This photograph shows a pageant of some type at Peace Dale Congregational Church. It would appear to be from the early 1920s based on the woman's hat in the back row and the length of the young girls' dresses. (Courtesy of Marise Sykes.)

This photograph was taken at Homestead Farm. Before the federal government condemned much of the Chase land, the farm extended to the shore of Narragansett Bay and included what is now called Melville. Laura and Milton Chase are flying kites down in the pasture of the "Old (George H. Chase) Homestead Farm." Note the railroad tracks and coaling facility at the Melville Fueling Station. A freshwater spring bubbled near the bungalow that served as a changing place for swimmers.

There were many family-owned apple orchards in Scituate in the early days. In the spring, the beautiful apple blossoms can still be seen on the remnants of the old orchards as well as on the orchards that remain in business today.

Memorial Day parades have traveled through Main Street in N. Scituate for many years and are still a popular event. This 1959 picture shows the Scituate Police Department, with Chief Jack Crowley, leading the parade.

The workers of the Narragansett Pier Railroad gathered in September 1906 for their annual clambake in the large paint shop across from the Peace Dale Train Station on Railroad Avenue. A special table had been built for the occasion to seat more than 100 railroad workers and their guests. The *Narragansett Times* reported that they dined on chowder, clams, bluefish, lobsters, sweet potatoes, brown bread, white bread, coffee, and watermelon, with cigars after dinner. W.A. Brown made the chowder, Elisha Gardiner supervised the clams' preparation, and "Photographer Rowsell secured some good pictures of the party while at dinner," *The Times* related in its October 5 issue. "Altogether it was the best time the railroad men have held for 20 years and the largest numbers present." (Courtesy of Pettaquamscutt Historical Society.)

This is the Centerdale village band, named the Young American Band, c. 1885. It was formed in August 1884 through the efforts of Frank C. Angell and George Cozzens. Although it started with twelve members, it grew to twenty-five members and was known as a flute and drum ensemble. Rehearsals were held in the basement of the Armory Hall, but the fire in that building in 1892 started the decline of the band, which disbanded in 1894.

The Hydraulion Engine & Hose Co. No.1 volunteers decked out one of their engines for the 1914 Fourth of July Parade. Thomas J. Goff said he believes the float is manned by John McGee, and the fellow in front by the tree is Domenic D'Ambricia, the barber.

Morrisey's Champs' Ringside Bar was located on Thames Street, c. 1910. It was typical of Bristol's numerous Thames Street "town pumps," with a brass rail, gas lights, cuspidors, and draught beer. These were popular watering holes for thirsty mill and dock hands; the Bristol Phoenix called such places: ". . . those low grog shops."

The Verdi Orchestra, conducted by Giuseppe Verdi, gave many concerts and was also part of a dramatic club. The band's specialty was playing songs native to the immigrants' hometowns in Italy. (Comm. Joseph R. Muratore Collection.)

Wearing the latest in swim-wear fashion, this happy group of ladies consented to have their photograph taken in 1905. With its natural, unspoiled beauty, the beaches on the island provided an excellent escape from the complex life of the city. (From the Henry A.L. Brown Collection.)

A clambake at Juniper Farm, August 2, 1891. The Cady family entertained many friends and townspeople at this gathering by the Kickemuit River.

This group of schoolchildren and their teachers posed on the front steps of Canonchet during a field trip there, c. 1895. Kate Chase Sprague started opening the mansion twice a week to the public. The tradition continued with Inez Sprague, Governor Sprague's second wife. This wonderful tradition was especially appreciated by schoolchildren who were exposed to one of the most remarkable buildings of its time. A charitable fund for children, also started by Inez Sprague, still exits today.

Narragansett House Guests, c. 1875. It was common for several related families to occupy a guest house at the same time. Often two and three generations of a family would vacation together. This wonderful photograph is an interesting study of such an occasion.

Four men serenade with instruments of the time. (Courtesy of *Westerly Sun* collection.)

This photograph shows players engaged in a lively reenactment of the capture of British General Richard Prescott, staged on July 11, 1927. The Newport Artillery Company stages the reenactment at an old farmhouse on West Main Road, south of Lawton Valley.

A view of the Johnston Theater in the early 1950s shows a lot of happy faces. Mario Votolato ran this theater on the second floor of the Ferri Block from about 1946 to the late 1960s. Mario's father, John, and later Mario operated a theater at Myrtle Hall from 1918 until 1942. The Ferri Block theater was run by Sid Richman and Bill Cappelli before Mario. (Photograph courtesy of Mario Votolato.)

A crowd is enjoying the Feast of Madonna Della Difesa in the late 1940s. This annual feast at Our Lady of Grace Church continues to play an important role in the Italian community. The parish was formed in 1912 and for many years held one of the largest festivals of Italian heritage in the local area. The feast attracted people from as far away as Canada. It continues today on a smaller scale. (Photograph courtesy of Eileen Perriello.)

The Hep Cat Canteen, held upstairs in the hall at the Manton Fire Station, is shown in the late 1940s or early 1950s. Mario Votolato, seen on drums in the rear, started the canteen at the request of Mrs. Barrett, who then took over and ran the canteen and a youth center for a number of years. (Photograph courtesy of Mario Votolato.)

Charlestown Beach cottagers wait for the mail at this beachside post office. Sending and receiving letters took on great importance when vacationers spent months at a time by the sea. (Courtesy Christine MacManus.)

These two young scouts, Scott Heinz and Daniel H. Brown, couldn't resist the lure of the huge Electric Company Diesel Engine, in August of 1978. The engine was being shipped to Block Island from the Point Judith Ferry Landing for the power plant. Thanks to the machine, life on Block Island in both summer and winter has become much more pleasant. (From the Henry A.L. Brown Collection.)

Students seek an explanation for Bressler's ousting at an April 1, 1940 meeting. In 1939, under newly elected Governor William H. Vanderbilt, the state was reorganized. The board of regents was abolished, and the college was no longer under James Rocket's department of education. The governor appointed a committee of top educators headed by President Henry Wriston of Brown to determine what would be required to take the state colleges out of politics. Seeing a breath of fresh air at the capital for the first time since 1935, Bressler pressed for exemption of faculty from state certification, return of budget surpluses to the college, authority to purchase supplies independent of the state purchasing department, a mill tax to support the college's financial needs, and university status for RISC. Bressler's ideas gained him strong support from the campus community. Wriston's committee, however, did not feel that RISC was anywhere near qualified to be a university, nor were new legislators eager to free the college from state control. The new board of trustees demanded fiscal accounting by Bressler. Bressler fought the trustees into 1940 and made excuses for not answering them. Seeing this as evidence of Bressler's bad faith, the trustees asked for his resignation by March 31, 1940, on the basis of fiscal ineptitude.

In 1908, under the direction of President Edwards, the new home economics department was organized. Its purpose was to give the young women of the state an equal opportunity with the young men to receive instruction in a vocational line. Helen Louise Johnson, a graduate of the Teachers College, Columbia University, New York, took charge of organizing and equipping the department. The course included work in house construction and its care, personal and public hygiene, textiles, preparation of food, and household administration. "It seeks to teach how to consume, as other vocational work seeks to teach how to produce."

In 1956, Robert Frost, the poet laureate of the United States, enthralled students at the new Memorial Union.

The entire student body took part in Cleanup Day, 1932. Here is a group grading the land near the football fields with Coach Frank W. Keaney, third from left, in charge. These were lean years, and economies had to be found where they could. Bressler found that by holding down expenditures and bringing more students in each year, he could lower the per-student cost to the state. In 1930, there were 646 students; after Bressler's first year, there were 814 students. Housing was scarce, so Bressler encouraged fraternities and sororities to build their own houses at their own expense.

An old-fashioned torchlight parade, in which more than 1,000 RISC students took part, touched off the opening salvo of the 1947 Pass the Bills campaign. The campaign sought favorable Rhode Island General Assembly support for two men's dormitories, a chemistry building, and a new gymnasium-armory. Over the years, grass-roots lobbying of this sort has been repeated again and again, up to the present day.

An old man and his gun—standing in front of his home. Typical Burrillville woodcutters at the turn of the century lived in sparsely-settled areas and made their living by hunting, fishing, and cutting wood. If supplies were needed, a walk to the nearest village was the order of the day.

Apponaug Railroad Station in 1898. Presidential candidate William Jennings Bryan is greeted by members of the Compston family during one of his "whistle-stops" in the campaign of 1898. The station played an important role in Warwick's history as troops left from here during the Civil War and during World War I. (Dorothy Mayor Collection.)

Sunday School at Hillsgrove in 1876. Thomas Jefferson Hill, like other mill owners of the nineteenth century, exerted his influence in nearly all aspects of village life. Shortly after he opened his iron works and mill in 1875, the village grew to forty-nine inhabitants. Hill used his influence and generosity to help establish the Hillsgrove United Methodist Church. This is the first Sunday school group at the church, c. 1876. (Hillsgrove United Methodist Church Collection.)

It's clambake time at the Old Stone Church, *c.* 1914. Old habits and good bakes don't die easily. For almost a century, the last Saturday in July was the day of the annual clambake. Bakemaster Jimmy Roies, assisted by his wife, Lisa, prepare their bake in the traditional Rhode Island fashion. About 2:45 p.m. on bake day, diners are invited to watch Jimmy and his helpers "pull the fire" and position the racks of food precisely over the red-hot stones and steaming ocean rock weed.

A street procession over fifty years ago. The Paper Box mill, as it was called, is in the distance. Sitting close to the Pocasset River that supplied its power, this small mill served the town well until it perished in a great fire several years ago. (Photograph courtesy of Mario Votolato.)

A crowd gathered at Myrtle Hall. The Popeye Club of 1939 was already twenty years old, and its membership was formidable. By now, of course, talking pictures were established, and even early color films had been shown on the authentic silver screen of Myrtle Hall.

Everybody came here. The hall was used for weddings, showers, banquets, minstrels—just about everything of a social nature. (Photograph courtesy of Mario Votolato.)

This 1926 photograph shows "Jack the Bunker," a notable Pawtucket resident who lived at the corner of Broadway and Margaret Streets. Jack kept pretty much to himself and wore the same clothes just about every day. A likable chap in every other respect, he allowed this photograph to be taken of himself, his stone house, white horse, and cow. (Foster collection.)

A turn-of-the-century headline in The *Newport Daily News* headline on May 31, 1899 read: "Newport's election celebration a complete success. Weather perfect, crowds immense and good-natured, decorations everywhere elaborate, parade an ovation to Sampson and his men . . ."

Stone Street, looking east, with the Bull House in the background. This photograph shows a float from a parade in 1912.

John O. Pastore (center) and St. Bartholomew parishioners. John O. Pastore, a former governor of Rhode Island and U.S. senator, was a vibrant, articulate man who once addressed the Democratic National Convention with the fire and passion of a TV evangelist! He is surrounded here by parishioners at the ground-breaking ceremonies for the St. Bartholomew Parochial School. (Photograph courtesy of St. Bartholomew Church.)

The St. Bartholomew Parochial School body. A great number of students are represented. The school is renowned for its excellence, and its students through the years have entered the finest high schools and colleges in the country. (Photograph courtesy of St. Bartholomew Church.)

A swarm of worshippers and the beloved statue of La Madonna Di Civita. To the believers, touching the statue is tantamount to touching the living person. Mixed here is all the faith, devotion, color, custom, and superstition of the ages. (Photograph from the collection of Joe Fuoco.)

Sutcliff Manufacturing Company's sixth outing at Rocky Point, on August 6, 1921. Located at 14 Leather Street (now running beside the Pawtucket Police Station and City Hall), it

was one of the largest commercial printing establishments in the state. In 1924 Sutcliff moved to Cross Street, in Central Falls, Rhode Island. (Courtesy of the *Times*.)

This dramatic presentation, believed to be from the 1890s, was entitled *Miss Jarley's Wax Works*. Kingston residents loved plays and musicals and were forever putting on one production or another on the lawn of the Kingston Free Library or at the home of Miss Robinson next door. There was a Little Rest Dramatic Club, and each August a production was put on to benefit the library. (Courtesy Pettaquamscutt Historical Society.)

Enjoying a game of pitching at the Jewish Community Center Carnival. Although they had schooling, both secular and religious, these children had time to play organized games or attend camps. The children of an earlier generation often had jobs after school; they found their recreation in ball playing in the neighborhood, and, in the winter, sliding on the more hilly streets.

A meeting in behalf of the Palestine Foundation Fund, 1928. The fund, which later became part of United Palestine Appeal, brought together Zionist organizations such as the Zionist

Organization of America, Labor Zionists, Hadassah, and Pioneer Women with non-Zionists to support, on a non-profit basis, immigration and settlement in Palestine.

Another look at the sprawling child population of the mill villages of Thornton, Pocasset, Simmonsville, etc. Saturday morning was the big day for these kids at the Myrtle Hall Theatre (still standing). They were all members of the Popeye club, which did not necessarily mean they liked their spinach. (Photograph courtesy of Mario Votolato.)

An outing in 1939. The Pocasset, Victoria, Priscilla, and the Atlantic Mills, etc. employed many of the mill workers in this photograph. Those who are not mill workers belonged to a very unique group of senators, store owners, etc. (Photograph courtesy of Rita Saccoccio.)

Two

To Serve and Protect

Disaster! An explosion and resulting $5 million fire enveloped O&R's Engine Shop shortly after 3 p.m. on October 15, 1948. All hands, Navy and civilian, instantly turned to rescuing trapped, injured, helpless personnel. (*Quincy Point Naval Air Station Volume II* by Sean Paul Michigan.)

The first line of defense against a growing Russian submarine menace in the North Atlantic was Quonset's and ComFair Quonset's Patrol Squadrons (VPs). Pictured here is the VP-7 crew on the ramp before Seaplane Hangar Two (their home) practicing a ditching drill before an over-ocean ASW patrol. (*Quincy Point Naval Air Station Volume II* by Sean Paul Michigan.)

Victory, Sweet Victory! Cheerful Marines greet the first plane to land on Guam, a Grumman TBF-1C Avenger torpedo bomber, after it was recovered from the Japanese on July 20, 1944. By this time, a large portion of Pacific Fleet carrier aviation had Quonset origins. A year later, half of the Carrier Air Groups that participated in victory flights over Tokyo Bay on the day of the Japanese surrender, V-J Day, had been formed or reformed at Quonset Point. (*Quincy Point Naval Air Station Volume II* by Sean Paul Michigan.)

Quonset's two Attack Carrier Air Groups, Korean War veterans CAG-3 and CAG-7, departed Quonset for the last time during the mid- to late 1950s as did most of Fairwing Three's elements except for VP-8 Hound Dogs. Quonset's focus now, with few exceptions, was Carrier Based Antisubmarine Warfare in the real world of the Cold War. Aboard the *Tarawa*, VS-31 S2F-1 SP-6 tensions up on port cat. (*Quincy Point Naval Air Station Volume II* by Sean Paul Michigan.)

As early as 1918, the General Board for Naval Affairs recommended that a seaplane base be established on Narragansett Bay, either at Newport or Quonset, to protect the Northeast from German submarine and surface ship attack. Had World War I continued into 1919, twin-motored machines, such as this Curtiss H-16 (complete with a Lewis gun), would have been assigned to the area. The lofty perch between the twin V-12 Liberty engines is manned by a Marine, while the waist gun position is handled by a sailor, c. 1918. (*Quincy Point Naval Air Station* by Sean Paul Michigan.)

Quonset's prime Cold War mission was support of the entire Anti-Submarine Task Group. (*Quincy Point Naval Air Station Volume II* by Sean Paul Michigan.)

After being trained at Quonset in the use of rockets and other air-to-ground weapons, VOF-1 was deployed aboard the USS *Tulagi* (CVE-72) for the Invasion of Southern France (Operation ANVIL DRAGOON). On August 16, 1944, officers in the squadron's ready room listen with rapt attention as squadron mate gives the lowdown on early, and highly successful, operations against the enemy. The especially intense gentleman with the coffee cup is Task Group Commanding Officer Rear Admiral Calvin T. Durgin. After Corsica was secured, he went on to do great things in the Pacific. (*Quincy Point Naval Air Station* by Sean Paul Michigan.)

Quonset's plane handlers and catapult crews were the unsung heroes at sea, performing some of the most dangerous jobs in the world. These crews of the USS *Tarawa* (CVS-40) prepare VS-31 S2F-ls for launch from "Building 40" amid deadly, close-coupled, whirling twin props that were a new phenomenon aboard ASW support carriers in 1955. (*Quincy Point Naval Air Station* by Sean Paul Michigan.)

In this April 1949 photograph, Quonset's VA-35 loads its TBM-3Es for deployment at the Carrier Pier. During the Truman administration, Douglas AD Skyraiders were in short supply, so venerable but obsolete World War II torpedo planes had to fill in. (*Quincy Point Naval Air Station* by Sean Paul Michigan.)

Reveille at the beginning of the day and retreat at sundown have for ages been part of American military tradition. The lowering of the flag at Fort Greble on July 24, 1921, was combined with a parade that followed the retreat ceremony, to which the families and children of garrison members and guests had been invited. Military and civilian dignitaries are seated to the left from where they will review the parading troops. (Jamestown Historical Society.)

From 1898 to well into the 1920s, Fort Greble was the site of much activity, with troops coming and going at all times. Capable of housing and sustaining a permanent cadre of 327 Coast Artillery Corps personnel in permanent barracks, the island facility could also accommodate transient militia and national guard units for short term training periods as needs arose. This photograph, taken in 1915, shows a group of men arriving. (Jamestown Historical Society.)

This photo shows members of the permanent garrison in formation during the summer of 1912. At that time the post housed the 14th, 109th and 110th Coast Artillery Companies, totalling 325 men and 9 officers. They were augmented by 413 R.I. National Guardsmen during the period from July 14 to July 21, and thereafter by 495 troops that arrived on July 21 and left on the July 28. Following the departure of the National Guard, the 109th and

110th Companies left for Fort Terry, New York, for camp and target practice. These troops shipped out aboard quartermaster steamers *Ayres* and *Branan*. The tall fire commander's station can be seen above left in the photograph, as can several of the officer's family quarters. The saluting gun and caisson are positioned near the flagstaff. (U.S. Army Military History Institute.)

Wearing white gloves, the Fort Greble Guard Detachment is being inspected in an area to the rear of the hospital building. A 6-man detail of performing buglers adds to the formality of the occasion. The guard house would be off the picture to the right. Based on the construction date of the hospital and the size of the trees, it is estimated the picture may have been taken in 1905. (Courtesy Joeseph E. Coduri.)

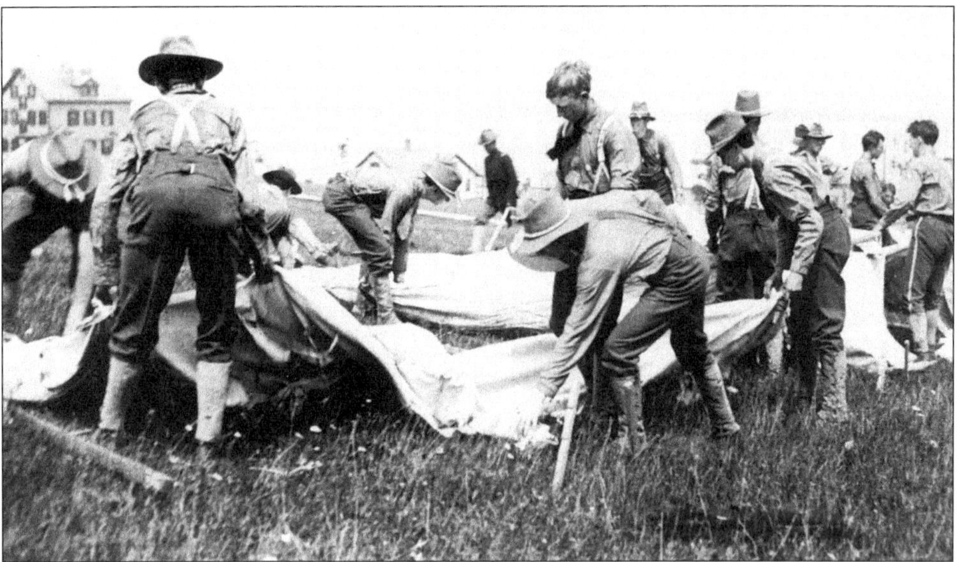

Putting up the large squad tents could be a chore. Here, the 1st Regiment of the R.I. National Guard is hard at work in April 1913. The tents were usually put up on the western side of the island, but this unit appears to be pitching theirs on the parade ground, based on their position in relation to the hospital, which appears in the picture. (Jamestown Historical Society.)

This "Seabee," the official symbol of Naval Construction Forces worldwide, was for many years positioned near the main entrance to the Naval Construction Battalion Center, Davisville, just off Route 1 in North Kingstown, Rhode Island. It was fabricated after a design by Frank Iafrate, a civilian worker at Quonset Point Naval Air Station. The "busy bee" carries the tools of the trade and a submachine gun, embracing the true spirit of these Navy men. The name "Seabee"—phonetically identical to CB (short for construction battalion)—was the logical name for this symbol, insignia, and that special group of Navy personnel. Iafrate himself signed on as a Seabee in 1942 and went through boot training at Camp Endicott. (Courtesy Carl A. Passarelli, EAC, retired.)

Bayonet training is a skill essential in hand-to-hand combat when an enemy has to be driven from his position by men on foot. Camp Endicott instructors, who at first seemed to be pretty human fellows, turned into fierce tigers charging their prey relentlessly during practice periods, as depicted here. (Collection of Virginia Dulleba.)

The above flag detail is from the 70th Naval Construction Battalion, a Seabee unit that assembled for training at Camp Endicott, Rhode Island. Here, battalion members received their boot training, which commenced on December 18, 1942. Following advanced training, some of the men deployed overseas as members of special pontoon detachments, where they became noted for their participation in the landings at Sicily, Salerno, and Anzio. Others saw service in Africa and the Pacific. (Courtesy Arthur Johnson, MMS 3/c.)

This photograph shows inspection time for the WAVES Detachment at Camp Endicott. The WAVES served the installation and the Seabees admirably by performing many essential administrative and personnel duty assignments, thus freeing up men for overseas and combat duty. (Collection of Virginia Dulleba.)

Here, a Pharmacist Mate is taking a blood sample from a worker. The pharmacy, which was located on the ground floor in Building 101, primarily served the military and their dependents. (Collection of Virginia Dulleba.)

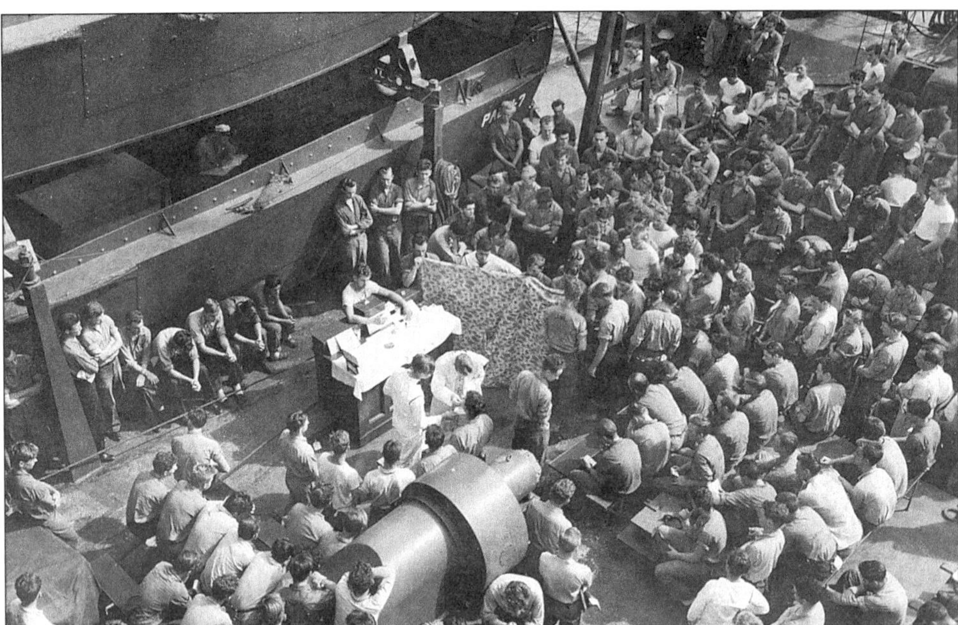

The 53rd NCB can be seen at Sunday religious services *en route* from Guam to Bikini in March 1946. Most of the old hands had been discharged soon after the war, so the unit was made up of many new Seabees who had little experience. With the guidance of a few good officers, some old-timers, and a real "can do" spirit, the outfit accomplished what it set out to do and more. (Courtesy Capt. John D. Burky, CEC, USN, retired.)

Torpedo practice, 1900. In its issue of March 10, 1900, the *Scientific American* documented torpedo practice launching in Newport waters. The torpedo boat is the *Morris* (TB-14). (Courtesy *Scientific American*.)

Members of the U.S. Naval Academy Class of 1864 at Newport, Rhode Island. When the U.S. Naval Academy was removed from Annapolis, Maryland, to Newport during the Civil War, classes went on, and these midshipmen became the first class to graduate during the academy's stay in Newport. (U.S. Naval Academy Archives.)

The president comes to Newport, 1906. President Theodore Roosevelt arrives for a naval conference in Newport. (Naval War College Museum.)

Preparing for a Saturday night dance. During World War II, the Jewish Community Center, Providence, held Saturday night dances for servicemen who were stationed in the Rhode Island area. Local girls volunteered as hostesses.

The first headquarters of the American Red Cross and Health Center, established in 1924 in the Frank O. Draper House at 204 High Street. This photograph was taken in 1932. (Courtesy of the *Times*.)

This photograph shows the kitchen in East Hall, 1910.

Veterans and sons of veterans are pictured in front of the old 1879 town hall in North Providence. This picture was taken c. 1901/02. Both Civil War and Spanish American War veterans are pictured. The person in the front row second in line beside the drummer is William F. Allison, a Civil War veteran who died at age 94 in 1925.

In June 1945, large patriotic crowds gathered at the T.F. Greene Airport at Hillsgrove to see the latest bombers and participate in patriotic military displays. The U.S. Army used the Hillsgrove facility for training fighter pilots. One of the units trained at Hillsgrove was called the "Checkertail Clan" and holds the distinction of being the first group in the U.S. Army Air Force to fight as a unit with an identifying logo. The airmen in this group, along with many others who spent time at the air facility, went on to serve with great distinction during the war. After the war, the Hillsgrove Airport was returned to the state. (Albert Ruerat Collection.)

Lifesaving Station and Crew, *c.* 1876. This station was established in 1876 on Narragansett Beach near the present site of the Dunes Club. Surf boats and equipment were stored on the first floor; crew quarters were located above in the second story. Pictured from left to right are Captain Benjamin Macomber, Daniel Billington, Horace Briggs, Terry Ralph, Thomas Sennett, Joshua F. Clarke, and William C. Chappell. Pictured with the crew is a "breech's buoy" which was used with a "lyle gun" to secure a lifeline to stranded vessels. The system had a 1/4-mile range, and crews would practice the technique to achieve two-minute response times. When the Life Saving Service merged with the Coast Guard in 1915, this system of rescue was maintained until the 1960s. In 1887, the Life Saving Crews of the Third District (Rhode Island and Long Island Sound) rescued "2,040 people from wrecks without the loss of a single life; a record that will probably never be equaled" (*Rhode Island: Genealogy-Biography, Vol. II*, 1908). The list of shipwrecks where crews from the District rendered assistance totals over five hundred, which attests to the high volume of maritime traffic and operating conditions in the nineteenth and early twentieth centuries. The Lifesaving Station on the beach was abandoned in 1888 when a new station was completed near the Narragansett Casino and Towers.

Sitting atop the 1936 Maxim, Captain Mike Placella and the fire dog, Sparky, present a familiar view in 1957 at the Thornton Fire Station. Manned at that time by volunteers, the station is still owned by the Thornton Volunteer Fire Association. (Photograph courtesy of Mike Placella.)

The Pawtuxet Volunteer Fire Company's 1949 Ford was painted all-white as opposed to the traditional red of other companies. (William Hall Library Collection.)

A steam-powered fire pumper on Washington Street. The first steam-powered fire engine was purchased by the city in 1806. In 1888, there were 124 firemen listed on the city coffers.

The first headquarters for the Rhode Island State Police in Glocester was in the Ben Steere house on Main Street at Douglas Hook Road across from Chepachet Grammar School. Glocester resident Ralph Bonat is on the left in this 1940s photograph. On this site today is Chepachet Union Church's Greenhalgh Hall.

The Geneva Volunteer Fire Company is pictured here *c.* 1927 at their new station on Douglas Avenue adjacent to Cushing Street. From left to right are: (front row) John Bargamian, Arthur Taylor, Bugar Brothers, Captain Allen, and Joseph Capobianco (driver); (back row) Walter Morrissey, ? Taylor, Joseph Celona Jr., Hatchedor Bargamian, and Eugene Benjamin.

Steam-powered fire engines were first made about 1859 and were widely used until the advent of gasoline-powered apparatuses in the early 1900s. The disastrous fire at the C.G. Bloomer and Company jewelry shop in the winter of 1891 caused the Pawtuxet Volunteer Fire Company to be formed. The company had 32 members and was the predecessor of all fire departments in Cranston. Their apparatus was a hose reel that they pushed in shifts. Albert Potter, president of the Rhode Island Company (the trolley car company), issued orders to the motormen to hitch the fire apparatus to the back of trolley cars. The trolley would then rush the apparatus to the area of the fire. In 1910 this fire company was the first motorized company in the state thanks to the trolley cars.

Three

Business and Industry

A new conveyance had arrived on the scene by the time this picture was taken at Maine's I Scream on Kingstown Road. In April 1906, W.G. Maine pledged to his patrons in the columns of *The Narragansett Times* that he would not increase the price of his ice cream "until he has consumed the two hundred and forty tons of ice he cut the past winter." (Courtesy Frank W. Smith Jr.)

The fruit counters of the First National Store on Main Street, Wakefield, overflow with bounty in this 1935 photo. The clerks are, from left to right: Alfred Joyal, George Cuttings, and LeRoy B. Kenyon. It was common for the fruit clerks to carry shoppers' purchases to their cars, because the fruit display was the last stop in the store. Mr. Joyal and Mr. Cuttings are deceased; Mr. Kenyon is retired after a long career with the supermarket chain, which eventually moved to Heritage Mall in the Dale Carlia Corner area. (Courtesy LeRoy and Eleanor Kenyon.)

The Columbia House's first floor became home to Archie Brown's motorcycle and bicycle dealership, which had been in a barn behind Brown's parents' house on Robinson Street, in the 1920s. This photograph shows Brown (left), an unidentified worker (behind doorway), and William E. Stedman. Shortly after this photograph was taken, Brown died of pneumonia and the worker (center) drowned in Silver Lake, according to Stedman's son, Everett Stedman. W. Luther Bates, who ran the stove shop in the adjacent space, also died suddenly while walking up Main Street. (Courtesy Everett Stedman.)

Henry Tucker is shown here with his pride and joy, potatoes. Tucker was among the first to farm potatoes on a large commercial scale in South County, according to his daughter, Marjorie Andre. Note the rows of chicken coops in the background, which belonged to Maurice Tucker. (Courtesy Marjorie Andre.)

The interior of a store selling meats, groceries, and fruits at 7 Child Street.

Mill workers in the weaving room. In 1847 the Warren Manufacturing Company constructed its first small stone mill on north Water Street, where it expanded in 1860 and 1873. Cutler Manufacturing began in 1869 and Parker Mills in 1879. The development of the textile industry presented new employment opportunities. In 1860 the town's population was 2,636. The addition of nearly one thousand new people between 1870 and 1875 reflects these changes.

Oystermen at the Massasoit Oyster Company.

A photograph showing a different area within the Peerless Soda Works, *c.* 1915. Besides Cobble Rock Ginger Ale, the company supplied area merchants and residents with another fine drink called PE-NE-TO. (Blackstone River Valley National Heritage Corridor Commission.)

Workers at Blount Seafood picking clams. Notice the Campbell's soup inspectors in the background against the right-hand wall.

The interior of R. Godin's Ice Cream Parlor and News Stand, *c.* 1910. Workers would often stop by, going to or coming from the mill, for an ice cream soda or a cigar. (Blackstone River Valley National Heritage Corridor Commission.)

Transporting the cotton goods from the mills was done by horse and wagon in the 1800s. This picture shows the finished cotton goods leaving the Ponaganset Mill.

The Peckham/Budlong Farm was originally one of the larger local farms, producing tons of hay as its main crop.

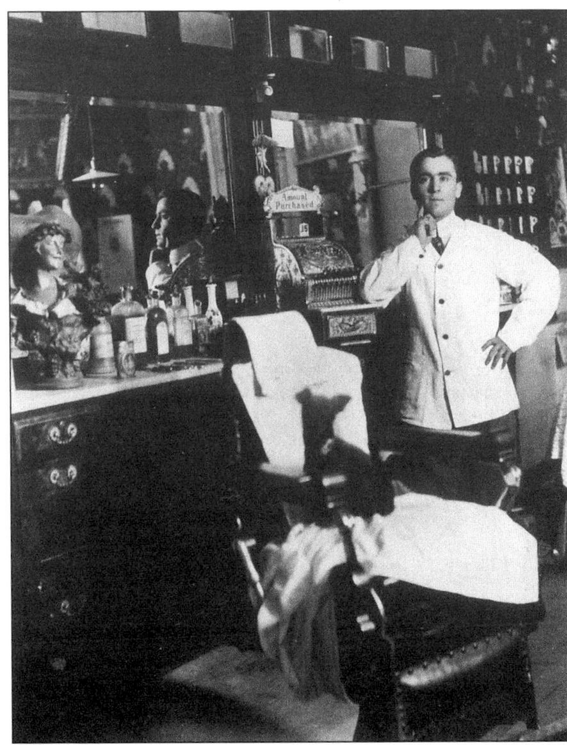

Lorenzo (Larry) Coletti appears in his barbershop at 1184 Atwood Avenue. Pictured here about 1920, Larry's Barbershop was on the first floor of a three-story tenement. Adjoining the shop was a poolroom. About 1925 he converted a garage on the property into a new barbershop. He died in 1981, aged ninety-two years, having run his shop until he was ninety. (Photograph courtesy of Anna Coletti Armstrong.)

An interior view of the hardware and paint store of the Wardwell Lumber Co., located on Thames Street, taken around 1903.

Founded on August 10, 1910, the Union Commercial Company is still in business at the same location, 479 Wood Street. Thomas Pansa, one of the original founders, is shown here in front of the counter; behind the counter is son Andrew A. Pansa, and today the store is run by Andrew Jr. Little physical change has taken place since this photograph was taken in 1936. The name Union Commercial came about by the "union" of five men from Atrani, Italy, who joined in establishing a "commercial" enterprise. Originally a grocery and grain store, inventory slowly expanded to include hardware, until—as can be seen here—the mix was about half and half: cans of paint share shelf space with bottles of olive oil and cans of tomato paste.

Homer Clarke delivered ice locally in his Ice Wagon for many years before selling out to Henry Jarvis, who continued the tradition.

These Oakland Mill workers were photographed in 1949. In 1987 the whole of Oakland Village received the distinction of being put on the National Register of Historic Places because of its visual conception of a typical mill village. From the 1890s onward, Oakland has changed very little in its appearance.

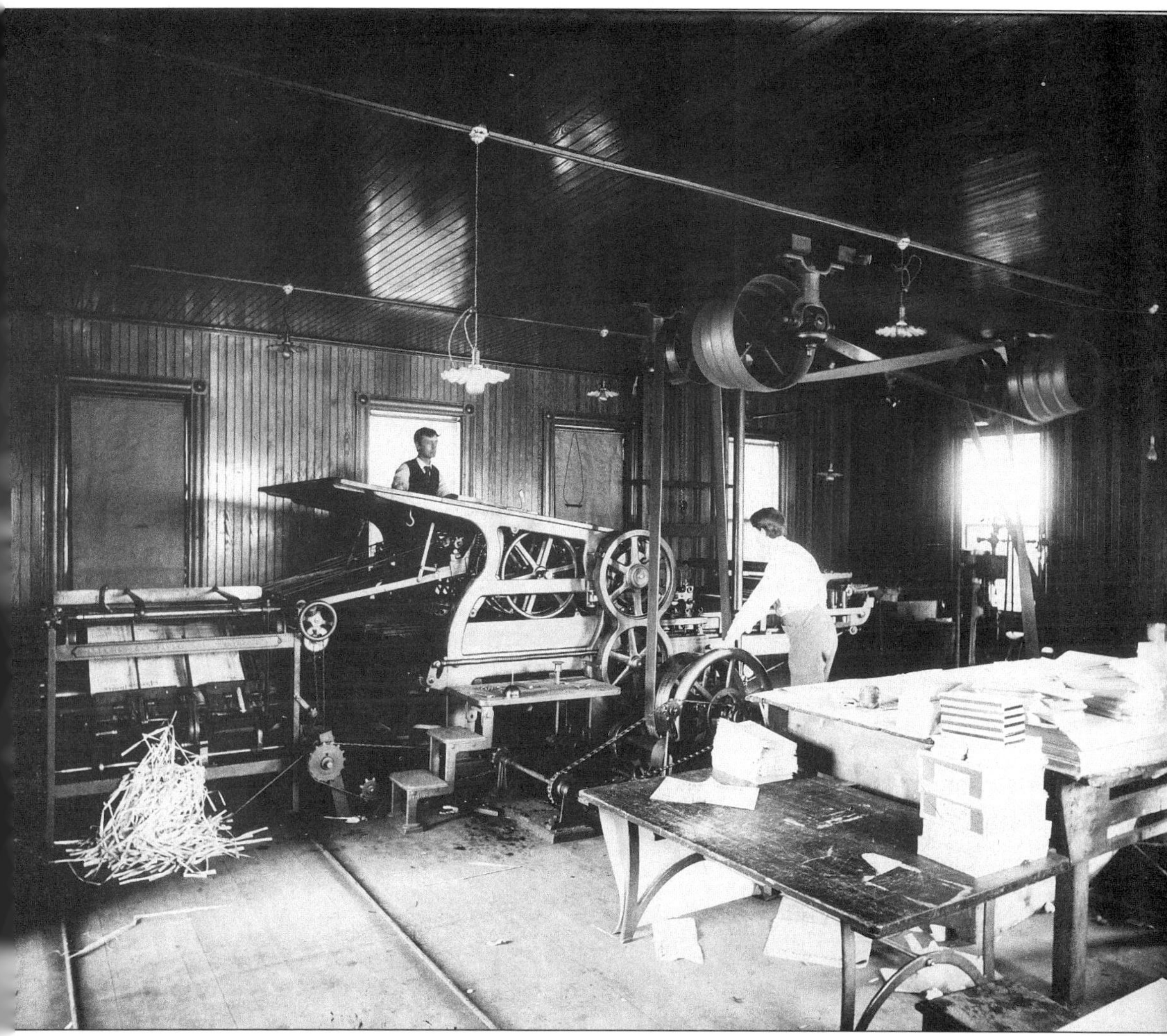

These presses were used in the printing of the *Pascoag Herald*, which was started in 1892 by Arthur S. Fitz. The *Herald* was a weekly newspaper which appeared every Friday without fail. Subscriptions cost $1 per year in 1894. The heavy presses were actually on the second floor of the Lincoln Mill Office; you can imagine the noise they must have made.

During World War I, the Universal Winding Company made hand grenades and other supplies for the allies. During World War II they made everything from parachutes to small machinery parts for the war effort. The Universal Winding Company foundry building was home to the Cranston Arms Company, which manufactured the Johnson Automatic Machine Gun (later rejected by the military in favor of the Garand rifle).

The cry of "rags" was a familiar one during the Depression as ragmen with their horses and wagons went about the city, trying to earn a few dollars for their families. In 1933, the Red Cross set up a "share your clothes" relief station at the Brick Store for the needy. They also passed out bags of flour from their headquarters at the Brick Store.

Jacques Lunch started out c. 1885 as Sullivan's Bar. In the early 1920s it became known as Jacques Lunch. Hughes and Leo Jacques are manning the counter in the photograph. Peter Rougas opened here as the Washington Lunch and continued until 1931, the year after the new bridge was built.

With so many hotels, restaurants, and clambake halls in Riverside, Edward Bowen saw a need for an icehouse to supply the tourist colony through the summers. He excavated an area near a brook on Willett Avenue and developed Bowen's Ice House and pond. Schoolboys would cut the ice in winter after school for around 10¢ an hour and load it by horse and wagon into the icehouse, which was built c. 1900. Mr. Bowen sold ice from the site and also delivered it by ice wagon throughout Riverside.

Soon after the restoration, visitors from all over the country began to arrive. In this photograph, delegates from the Virginia Chamber of Commerce pose in front of the renovated historic structure. The mill had been radically altered, and all parts of it had been rebuilt, including the fenestration.

Dean Company Picnic in 1918. During the early twentieth century, outings and picnics were common, especially around the Fourth of July. Employees of the George H. Dean Company gathered in front of the armory at 3259 Post Road on the way to an outing along the shore. On the facade of the building are the words "Kentish Artillery," with the dates 1797 and 1912. The first date indicates the founding of the Kentish Artillery and the date of the building of the wooden armory. This burned in the fire of 1911 and the brick structure, now the Warwick Museum, replaced it in 1912. Note the cobblestones, the streetcar tracks, and the absence of Saint Barnabas's Church, which also burned in 1911. (Phyllis Dean Collection.)

During the early 20th century, farming was the major occupation on the island. Ezebiel Rose, son of Peggy and Caleb Rose, is displaying his newly sharpened sickle-bar in preparation for cutting hay on Block Island in 1916. Note the barefoot boy, with cheeks of tan, holding the reins. (From the Henry A.L. Brown Collection.)

Some hard-working fishermen take a smoke break near a shanty at Old Harbor, c. 1910–1915. In an earlier period, fish were carried through the sand to the fish houses. Obviously, this was very hard work. (From the Henry A.L. Brown (G.K. Page) Collection.)

Early 20th-century lobster fishermen, with their catch at the Old Harbor break-wall, c. 1912, enjoy the benefits of the sea. The waters off Block Island, just 10 miles from the Rhode Island mainland and 18 miles from Montauk Point, have proved to be an ideal setting to catch tuna, marlin, and swordfish, as well as lobster. (From The Henry A.L. Brown (G.K. Page) Collection.)

The pumphouse and crew of the Old Jointa Rock Hole. The crew posed for this picture in the late nineteenth century. By that time, the quarrying and burning of limestone was already a 240-year-old industry in Limerock. Initially begun as a part time occupation to supplement farming income, demand for the limestone eventually made its production an important local industry. (Everett Wilbur.)

In this photograph, workers leave the east gate of the Peace Dale Manufacturing Co. Workers in the Peace Dale mills were considerably better off than in some textile concerns, but the "operatives," as they were called, still toiled for much less money than the supervisors and lived a life that was tightly controlled by the company, which owned their housing and deducted store bills from their pay. At the time of the 1906 strike, the *Narragansett Times* reported the weekly payroll to be about $6,500, or an average pay of $9 a week. The disparity in pay was noted by Peter Crawford Stewart in his 1962 master's thesis, "A History of the Peace Dale Manufacturing Co." In the 1880s, he noted, the average mill worker made between $1 and $1.50 a day while overseers made $2 to $5 a day and supervisors were paid between $4,000 and $10,000 a year. (Courtesy of Pettaquamscutt Historical Society.)

This photograph shows haying time at the Potter homestead on Potter Lane. The Potters employed a retinue of servants, chauffeurs, and farmhands and were among the wealthiest residents of Kingston. (Courtesy Pettaquamscutt Historical Society.)

Henry Green (wearing the top hat) in front of his clothing store, Providence, *c.* 1870. Henry Green, who came to Providence in 1856, opened his first store, a tailor shop, on North Main Street. Over the years he changed his line of business to mens' clothing and in the process moved his establishment several times to locations on North Main Street, to Market Square, and finally to Dorrance Street near city hall. (Courtesy of Temple Beth El Archives.)

Adler's Army and Navy Store, Wickenden Street, Providence, 1924. Fred Adler was an engraver who worked in the jewelry industry. Since this work was seasonal and unpredictable, he opened a clothing store. During the Depression years, Adler went to the jewelry factories seeking engraving work, which he would bring back to his store to complete when not waiting on trade.

The Builders and Makers, *c.* 1897. This large group of workmen have gathered on the northeast corner of the "new" Mathewson Hotel to record its last modification. The huge work force required to "rebuild" hotels during the off-season provided steady work for hundreds of local men. Construction of cottages and other business establishments in Narragansett proceeded with little interruption for the next twenty years. However, by 1900, the boom in hotel construction had peaked.

Shown here is Emma Baron in the doorway at 2007 Smith Street, which was at the left end of the F.C. Angell building. Baron was the postmistress from 1910 to 1915 when her brother Charles succeeded her. At that time, a person could not make a living running a post office, so the post office was usually part of another business.

This is the Herbert H. Sweet Livery Stable near the Centerdale Mill. In recent years, a Christmas shop and Salvation Army were located at this site. Today, the site is a vacant lot. In this early twentieth-century photograph, from left to right are: Herbert H. Sweet, Barney McNally, Dennis Mackie, Pat McNally, and Billy Favreau. This land is still owned by a Sweet family grandson, Herbert Sweet.

A group of neighborhood people gathered in front of the Kirby Store *c.* 1910. This store and home were located on the corner of Metcalf and Woonasquatucket Avenues. Michael J. Kirby purchased this lot in 1908 and built the store and tenement. The 1910 North Providence Directory lists the store at 127 Woonasquatucket Avenue and Kirby's home at 9 Metcalf Avenue.

Employees of the E.R. Vieira Coal and Wood Company. Kneeling in front is Joseph Botelho. Standing, from left to right, are Bill Theroux, Alfred Vieira, Manuel Guimary, Emeziah Gorton, and Joe Godena. The company was a family-owned business for almost six decades, from 1922 until it was sold in 1981, and was one of the oldest and most respected family businesses on the island.

A.E. Ventrone was a prominent wholesale grocer and importer of Italian products. He was the first person to establish a chain of grocery stores on Federal Hill and nearby. He introduced many Italian food products to the United States. His place of business was located at 248 Atwells Avenue in Providence. He was a pioneer in the mass distribution of products through horse and wagon delivery. (Comm. Joseph R. Muratore Collection.)

The display area of the Scialo Brothers Bakery, located at 257 Atwells Avenue in Providence, features examples of the fancy pastry and wedding cakes that have been baked by the Scialos since 1916. In the photograph are Giuseppe Gaeta, Carol (Scialo) Gaeta's father-in-law, Jennie Falola, and three other employees. (Comm. Joseph R. Muratore Collection.)

The interior of Jennie's Ice Cream Parlor is shown here. Jennie Amalfitano was a gold-star and a two-time blue-star mother: her son Anthony was killed at the Battle of the Bulge in Europe. Note the prices for the ice cream specialties—15¢ for a sundae! (Comm. Joseph R. Muratore Collection.)

This photograph shows Alfred C. Schmidt when he was proprietor of what is now the Kingston Hill Store. Note the Jell-O mold advertisements in the window. (Courtesy of Pettaquamscutt Historical Society.)

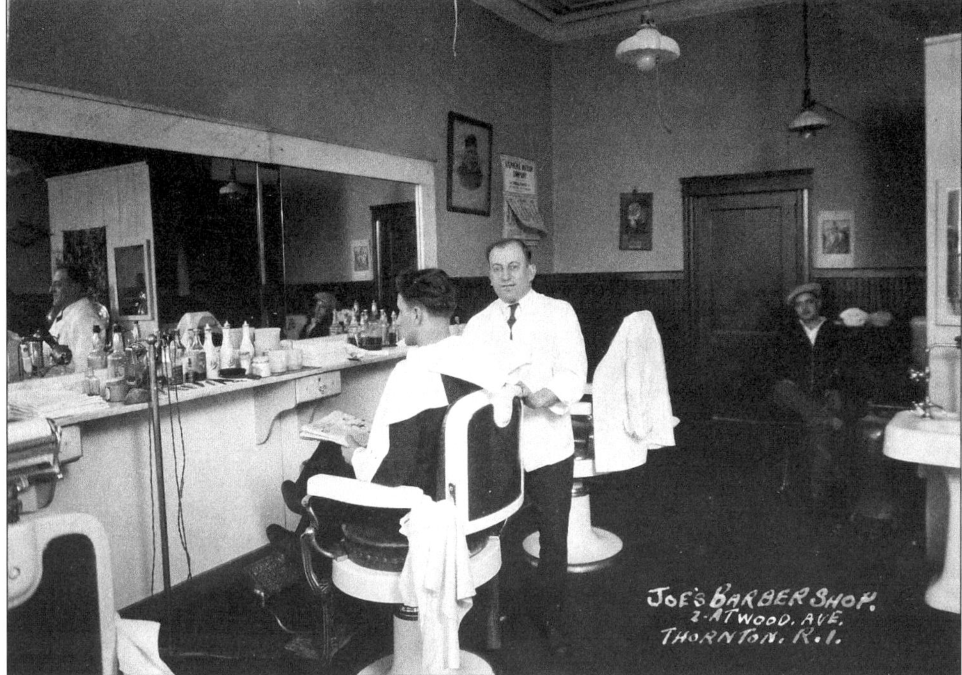

Essential as coal and water. There was never a shortage of barber shops in any mill village. Joe Croce in a spiffy shop on Plainfield Street stops for a pose while cutting a young man's hair. Notice the white bottles on the counter, unquestionably the tart, strong smelling preference of the day, Old Spice. (Photograph courtesy of Joe Croce.)

The big night in Olneyville, a Saturday night dance. Notice the harmless refreshments listed, even cola with a "K." (Photograph courtesy of the Nickerson Community Center.)

Long Wharf. The Newport Water Works and some of its employees are shown here, c. 1884.

The corner of Green and Thames Street. The Kinsey Building was built to house the National Bank of Rhode Island. It is shown here with some of the construction crew, c. 1892. (Courtesy of the Newport Historical Society.)

This 1884 picture, by photographer C.L. Littlefield, shows the shops in the Dexter Block, at what was then 138-142 Main Street, next to the Wheaton-Toole Building. The Dexter Block was built by Pawtucket's Nathaniel G.B. Dexter in 1865. William H. Taylor sold boots, shoes, hats, and caps, next to George C. Gates, the boot maker. On the right was Ruel S. Darling & Sons, a grocery and meat market. (Courtesy of the *Times*.)

Pullano's and Sons Market in Silver Lake. Those who could, who had the talent, the trade, and the opportunity, not to mention the sheer courage, opened up their own businesses. Note the stocked shelves! To the left are the words, "Good Friday, April 7, 1939." Notice the absolute cleanliness and neatness of this village market.

Four
TRANSPORTATION

Within a stone's throw of the Narragansett Pier Railroad tracks was a budding new form of transportation. Archie Brown (left) and William E. Stedman sold Indian motorcycles and bicycles from a barn behind Archie's parents' house at Robinson Street and Woodruff Avenue. This photograph was probably taken about 1916, before Brown moved the business to the first floor of Columbia House. (Courtesy Everett Stedman).

Elmer E. Crandall was the first free delivery rural postman to work out of the Peace Dale Post Office. In 1915, according to the South Kingstown and Narragansett street directory, he lived on North Road in Peace Dale. (Courtesy of Pettaquamscutt Historical Society.)

On March 1, 1902, this Narragansett Pier Railroad passenger train derailed about a quarter of a mile east of the Kingston Junction; it was the worst accident the railroad had met with up until that point. Heavy rain the previous night had eroded the track, which gave way as the train crossed over it. The coal tender and two cars ran off the tracks first as the rails broke, and then the engine jumped the track. A crowd gathered as a wrecking train attempted to raise the train back onto the tracks. No one was injured, and the passengers and baggage were taken to the station by carriage. Remarkably, reported the *Narragansett Times*, "Not a window in the whole train was broken." (Courtesy of Pettaquamscutt Historical Society.)

Members of the Barbour family of Avondale have donned their Sunday best for a turn-of-the-century partyboat excursion in a stately wooden launch. Summer residents could readily avail themselves of the numerous partyboats that operated out of Watch Hill Cove throughout the season. A huge gaff sail, replete with three tiers of reefing points, luffs calmly in the summer breeze on the catboat that lies astern of the power launch. The snapping Union Jack on the bow of the Barbour's craft denotes either a Sunday outing or a holiday. (Courtesy of Dwight Brown Jr.)

Captain Frank H. Robinson first steamed up the Pawcatuck River in the new tug *Westerly No. 2* on March 21, 1912. Built to tow barges up and down the river, the *Westerly No. 2* also made passenger excursions to the likes of Block Island, Rhode Island, and Greenport, New York. This sturdy tug served until January 24, 1932. In this 1913 winter scene, *Westerly No. 2* is breaking ice on the Pawcatuck. (WHS.)

A family poses while out for a carriage ride in the early 1900s. (Courtesy of George H. Utter collection.)

A fine team, wagon, and driver wait in front of 47 and 49 Elm Street. (GHU)

Old Home Week parade in 1900. Vanderbilt sent a contingent of wagons to represent Oakland Farm in the parade. Seen here on Farewell Street are four of Oakland's teams: (first wagon) driver J. Fred Sherman, Billy Adams, and superintendent of Oakland Farm Alee Adams; (second wagon) driver Frank Goncalves and herdsman Henry Mills; (third wagon) driver William Gifford and Harry Groom; (fourth wagon) driver Manuel Freitas and Ed Saddington.

Car 29 of the interurban Newport and Fall River Street Railway at Tallman Switch at the top of Park Avenue, *c.* 1900. The trolley car has stopped to oblige the photographer before swinging onto East Main Road for its run to Newtown and beyond.

Delivery truck #2 of the Peerless Soda Works *c.* 1915. The soda company, owned by J.B. Lambert, made a variety of carbonated beverage drinks. (Blackstone River Valley National Heritage Corridor Commission.)

The Auburn & Eden Park Trolley, c. 1900. This trolley car was known as a "bloomer" because it was open during the months of pleasant weather. Notice the boy who took the opportunity to make some personal history. The Elmwood trolley traveled to Roger Williams Park, a pleasant place to hear a band concert or just enjoy a quiet stroll about the park on a Sunday.

Old Port Days on the Point in 1925. The building in the background is the Dennis House, built in 1740. For the celebration, residents on the Point dressed in colonial costumes and many of the houses were open to display antiques and family heirlooms.

Stagecoach driver Stephen Knowles waits for passengers in front of the Joe Reynolds Tavern, probably during the time it was operated by John N. Taylor. Knowles met all trains at the Kingston Station with his coach. The railroad bypassed the village when it was constructed in 1837. When the Narragansett Pier Railroad was launched in 1876, creating a direct rail link between the Kingston Station and the resort at Narragansett Pier, the real decline of the stage routes began. The stage ceased to run a year after the Narragansett Pier Railroad began. (Courtesy Pettaquamscutt Historical Society.)

The Commercial Parade on the Fourth of July, 1917, aroused citizen's patriotism during World War I. F.W. Woolworth's Five & Ten Cent Store, at 242-244 Main Street, is in the background. The New England Bakery, founded by Henry J. Blais and the bakers of Bamby Bread, became the Ward Bakery. (Courtesy of the *Times*.)

A Pawtucket water fountain, ably designed for both man and beast (note the drinking cups for small animals at the base). (Courtesy of the *Times*.)

The Pawtucket Express, which everybody caught for rides to Providence, loading up on East Avenue at the corner of Main Street, *c.* 1940s. (Pawtucket Public Library.)

A trolley moving none-too-swiftly along the tracks on Dyer Avenue. This trolley was a former horse car that carried passengers from as far, in those days, as Swan Point and Butler Avenue on the East Side of Providence to Dyer Avenue. (Photograph from the booklet *The Rhode Island Company*.)

Serving as a conductor in the late nineteenth century was no job for the weak, as conductors stood at the front end of their vehicles, exposed to the weather. These conductors, dressed to face the elements, are getting ready to leave Pawtuxet in 1897/98 for Union Station. (From the Henry A.L. Brown Collection.)

A horse and buggy wait in front of the Fiske Homestead at Herald Square in Pascoag in 1894. James Fiske owned the Sheffield Worsted Mills, later known as the Anchor Mills. The unknown driver was the chauffeur for Mr. Fiske. Bradford Court housing for the elderly is currently located on this site.

A horse and sled on Laurel Hill were photographed in the snow in the early 1900s. In 1888 one of the heaviest snowstorms ever hit with major force. Even the trains became helpless, and an engine got stuck in a snow bank near the Oakland Station.

The first trolley to come to Chepachet arrived on June 30, 1914. Posing for the photographer are (in front) Frank Davis in a straw hat; the boy and girl are George and Dorothy Hopkins. Frank Potter, in a straw hat, stands behind Cora Shippee on the steps. Jennie and Cora Greenhalgh are seated inside with elbows out the windows. Deforest Richmond stands under the porch at the store.

A Pony Cart for the Children, *c.* 1895. Local stables maintained a variety of livery for any occasion. These fun-loving children might be on their way to the beach or the Narragansett Casino, or just a drive to the countryside.

Mary Geers tells us that her uncle can be seen on this horse-car, which made its way on Block Island in 1911. The vehicle is stopped before the Cassius Clay Ball House, "Harbour Cottage," at the major intersection at Old Harbor. The horse-car was used each summer for 15 years and ran between Old Harbor, Crescent Beach, and New Harbor. (From the Henry A.L. Brown Collection.)

Now that car was something, the talk of the town. This was the famed intersection of the village of Thornton, and the building behind it was the first "Mall." It housed a bowling alley, two barber shops, a deli-spa, a pool parlor, and an espresso coffee shop on the first floor; on the second floor was one of the two motion picture theatres in the village. The people here are Mike Leo (left), the owner of the pool parlor, and Mike Rainone (right), the proud owner of the convertible. (Photograph courtesy of Joe Fuoco.)

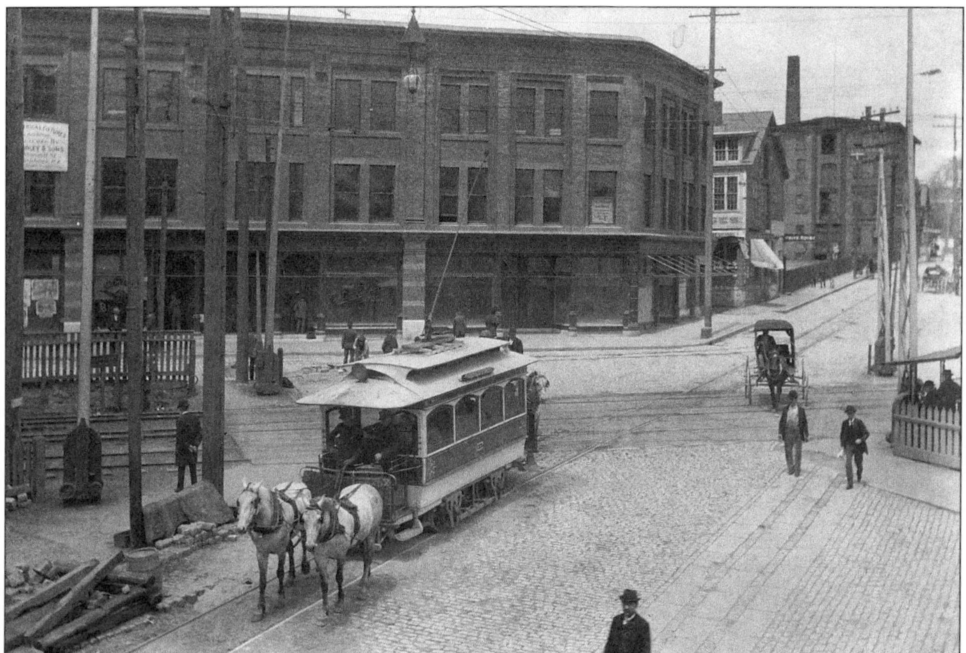

In-town transportation. By the latter part of the nineteenth century, mass transportation by horse-drawn and electric means had become available in the more thickly-settled areas of the Lower Blackstone Valley. (BVHS.)

Driving excursion, Cumberland Hill. The novelty of motoring is explored by these men who were photographed by A.L. Sherman driving around the area of Cumberland Hill on a Saturday afternoon in 1908. (BVHS.)

This omnibus was hustled into service during the great trolley strike of 1902 in Pawtucket. Half stagecoach and half horsecar, the wagon was operated by striking motormen and conductors, who kept the 5¢ fares for the union's welfare fund.

This photograph captures the chaos of sewer and track construction on Main Street in Pawtucket in 1891. The installation of street railway tracks interrupted urban travel the same way road repairs do today.

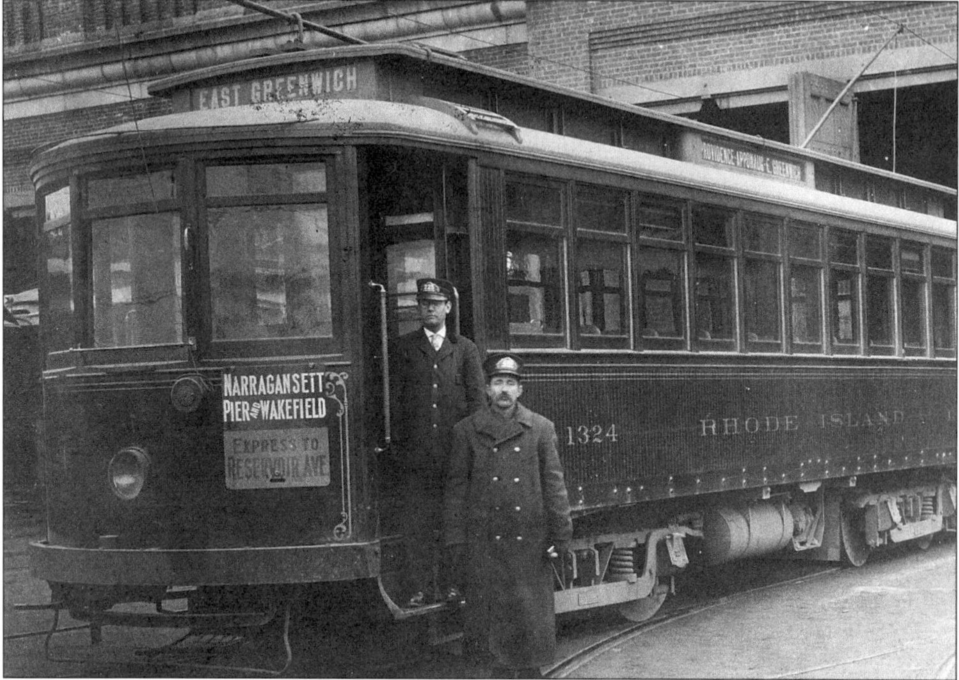

A trip to Rhode Island's South County shoreline was worth the cost of a ride alone. The Narragansett Pier streetcar passed through suburban Warwick, East Greenwich, Wickford, and Wakefield to the beautiful beaches of Narragansett. Employees pose at the Elmwood carbarn in 1912.

Less charming in the snow is downtown Providence. The trolley plow clears the way for an Arlington streetcar at Washington and Empire Streets.

The trackless trolley, or trolley bus, appeared in Rhode Island beginning in 1931. The Pullman coach in Exchange Place is a later version.

Service to Crescent Park, known as the Coney Island of the East, began at the dawn of trolley service. This bloomer, with a toddler aboard, featured canvas awnings that blocked the sun, but not the summertime breeze. Small stained-glass panels decorated the very top of the streetcar and colored the incoming light as red, white, and blue.

Material moved in two directions along railway tracks. Here, a delivery wagon loads products onto a suburban car to Buttonwoods in Warwick. In this case, passengers probably took up more room than crates and boxes. A photographer snapped this shot in front of the train station in downtown Providence. Notice the middle-class attire of the women.

Four
THE COAST

Looking north from Lighthouse Point, which was acquired from George Foster in 1806 for $500, a turn-of-the-century viewer would witness East Beach, its pounding surf, and the relatively undeveloped shoreline. (GHU-Burdick.)

Looking west toward Napatree Point, note the restricted attire for the ladies. One longtime summer visitor remembered, "I wore a black, very full dress belted at the waist, very full shirred skirt that came down over my knees, and long black stockings with garters at the top and black sneakers . . . we were very, very discreetly clad . . . we didn't show any more of our skin than we did when we were on the street" (*Life's Little Pleasures*). (GHU-Burdick.)

The Bathing Hour, *c.* 1890. The most popular time to "bathe" was between 11 am and 1 pm. At such times there were often over a thousand bathers in the water and double that number watching from the balconies or shelters that fringed the beach.

The Simeon Whitford family reposes on the porch of Moonstone Cottage, located just west of the end of Moonstone Beach Road in South Kingstown. Seated is Simeon Whitford. His oldest daughter, Hannah, shown standing beside him, was the grandmother of Everett Hopkins, who recalls his mother saying that his grandfather, John Hopkins, named the cottage—and thus the beach— "Moonstone," because at night the full moon glittering on the pebbles made them look like the jewel of the same name. John Hopkins, like his grandson, was a teacher and at one point taught at a Narragansett Indian school. He eventually sold the cottage and bought property at Moonstone Beach Road and Matunuck Schoolhouse Road he dubbed "Little Moonstone Camp." An icehouse was located to the north of this cottage on Card's Pond and the family had seaweed rights to the shore. Seven cottages at Moonstone Beach, including this one, were destroyed during the Hurricane of 1938; today the land, save one lot to the east, is part of the Trustom Pond National Wildlife Refuge. (Courtesy Everett Hopkins.)

Narragansett Pier was always one of the more fashionable resorts along the South County coast. These bathers gathered on Sunday, August 10, 1902, according to a date on the back of the photograph. The beach may have been crowded that day because about 600 "excursionists," or day-trippers, had arrived in the Pier that day from Providence aboard the steamer *Warwick*. In the background of this photograph are the bowling alleys of Webster and Baur, run that season by William Cosgrove of Blackstone. Among the summer visitors who had recently arrived, according to *The Narragansett Times*, were John H. Holmes, owner of the *Boston Herald* and his son, John H. Holmes Jr., in town to watch the polo matches, and his employee J.J. McNamara, who was covering the tournament. A West Virginia senator and Bishop Thomas Conaty of Washington also had recently arrived to stay at the Imperial. (Courtesy Judith Babcock.)

Halsey C. Herreshoff, navigator aboard the successful 1980 America's Cup defender *Freedom*, is the grandson of Nathanael G. Herreshoff; he is a naval architect and president of the Herreshoff Marine Museum and the America's Cup Hall of Fame. (*Providence Journal* photograph.)

The Steel Frame of the *Rainbow* under Construction in the South Shop of the Herreshoff Yard, March 1934. The *Rainbow* was plated with steel above the water line and bronze below. After beating the *Yankee* by a narrow margin in the trials, the *Rainbow* lost the first two Cup races to the English *Endeavour I*, which was sailed by owner-skipper Thomas Sopworth, an aircraft manufacturer.

The *Columbia* (foreground) and the *Shamrock II*, 1901, shown just before the 5-minute gun, are seen jockeying for the best position. The *Shamrock II* was considered to be a considerable foe to challenge for the Cup held by the New York Yacht Club for 50 years. (*Leslie's Weekly* photograph.)

Sir Thomas Johnstone Lipton and Captain Wringe on the Bridge of Lipton's Steam Yacht, the *Erin* (formerly the *Aegusa*), c. September 1899. Lipton purchased the *Erin* at a cost of $375,000, for the purpose of convoying the *Shamrock* to America for its challenge, according to the *Boston Sunday Journal* of September 24, 1899.

Although a member of the Royal Ulster Yacht Club, Sir Thomas was not a yachtsman. His challenge, it was widely reported, was due wholly to his determination to keep the name of Lipton before the world.

The wooden yacht *Intrepid*, designed by Olin Stephens, is shown receiving a sail from her tender, the *Bystander*. The *Intrepid* had a radically changed hull profile from previous 12-meter yachts. She easily defeated the three American contenders in the trials and the challenger, *Dame Pattie*, four times straight in the Cup races.

Surf and sand, and lovely linen-clad Misses are seen here, *c.* 1910. Readers familiar with Dubois's photographs know that he often employed his daughters as models. These two girls appear in several of Dubois's seaside photographs.

Henry Littlefield (far right) and his friends are aboard his fishing boat, the *Madilene*, in 1934. The group was about to leave Old Harbor in pursuit of a sensational trip, hopefully resulting in a catch of fish. This sturdy vessel survived the Hurricane of 1938. (From the Sandy L. Strickland Collection.)

This aerial view of Narragansett Pier shows the area just east of the Towers. The landscape is almost unrecognizable because of urban renewal, but one landmark that still remains is the Narragansett Post Office at the top right. (Courtesy Daryl Anderson.)

Farmer Charles Henry Crandall (second from left) harvests seaweed on the Weekapaug shore with help from hired hand George Rathbun (standing on wagon). Crandall, the author's great-grandfather, used the seaweed to fertilize potatoes and corn on his District No. 6 farm in Westerly. The Crandalls were among several farmers who had seaweed-gathering rights written into their deeds. Crandall's grandson, Frank H. Crandall Jr., recalls his father telling him that competition among the farmers to gather the seaweed was fierce; after seaweed had been washed ashore by a storm, the farmers would cover their horses' hooves in burlap so other farmers would not hear them making their way to shore. The seaweed was spread on the fields in the fall and then plowed under in the spring after it had decayed. Descended from one of the town's original founders, Charles Henry Crandall was a prominent member of the Westerly community, active in Republican politics, and respected for his thriving trapping and farming enterprises. When he died in 1932, *The Westerly Sun* noted, "There was perhaps no man better known throughout southern Rhode Island and eastern Connecticut than the deceased." (Courtesy Dorothy Crandall Bliss.)

Two people enjoy a sail, probably on Point Judith Pond. Carefree days on the pond have started many a love affair with South County. (Courtesy Daryl Anderson.)

Six
Places

The Providence-Johnston border ran down the Woonasquatucket River and then across the western side of Olneyville Square, shown here about 1900. Most of the buildings in the foreground were in Johnston including, on the left, Johnston's town hall. From 1870 to 1886 the town rented space for town offices in the Irons Block. (From R.L. Wonson Collection.)

Pictured here is the Tiverton approach to the Sakonnet River Railroad Bridge, c. 1906. The Fall River to Newport run of the Old Colony and Newport Railroad ran through some of the most scenic country in Bristol County. Over the years the line was operated by the New York, New Haven and Hartford Railroad, and later the Penn Central Railroad.

The dirt Harbor Road is pictured here, c. 1905. Local tradition maintains that Adamsville was a minor port and maintained a snug harbor in the 18th and early 19th centuries. This is documented by the Blaskowitz map of 1777, which shows the Acoaxet River navigable to Adamsville.

In the 1880s, Watch Hill Cove was guarded by a skyline of rambling wooden structures that included the following, from left to right: the flag-bedecked Plimpton House and Annex; the three-chimneyed Narragansett House; an unidentified cottage; the north wing of the Ocean House; the steepled Watch Hill Chapel; the two-tier porches of the Atlantic House; and the vast Watch Hill House, beneath Old Glory. Prior to the advent of trolley traffic in 1894, Watch Hill was mostly accessible by water. In the earlier days, sailboats such as the *Fanny Golden* and *North Star* sailed between Westerly and Watch Hill with passengers. In later years, the 105-foot sidewheel steamer *Sadie* sailed between Westerly and Watch Hill and the awning-covered *Watch Hill* steamer, depicted in the center foreground of this photograph, sailed regularly between Stonington, Connecticut, and Watch Hill. Early deeds refer to Watch Hill Cove as Pawcatuck Bay, Pawcatuck River, and Wilcox Cove. (GHU-Burdick.)

Pictured here is Bay Street, formerly known as the Midway. Note the inviting porches of the Columbia House in the right center and the trolley tracks that run from north to south in this 1919 photograph. Also, note the fact that all of the automobiles parked on both sides of Bay Street are pointing in the same direction. (WHS.)

Looking north on Bay Street from the carousel, this bustling intersection with Larkin Road was a popular amusement center during the 1920s. Note the "WLIN" of the Larkin bowling alley sign to the right of the automobile. One resident recalls that he "bowled there so often that he knew the alley well and it was easy to make 10 strikes in rapid succession" (*Seaside Topics*, September 1942). (WHS.)

A mid-1950s Fourth of July parade makes a hard turn east up High Street. Crowds that came to view the parade during the 1950s and '60s usually numbered between thirty-five and fifty thousand. In the twenty-five years since the bicentennial celebration and parade, crowds have seldom numbered less than one hundred and fifty thousand, and Bristol Harbor is always choked with pleasure craft during the celebration. In the center foreground of this aerial view is the Raymond DeLeo estate; in the center is the Lobster Pot Restaurant; and at the far right is the former Nathaniel Herreshoff residence, known as "Love Rocks."

On January 27, 1895, most of the college's students were attending the Kingston Congregational Church when a fire broke out in College Hall. The fire started in a closet near a chimney. Within an hour it destroyed the building, while onlookers watched helplessly. Kingston had no fire department. The fledgling college had no insurance, and $12,000 worth of equipment was lost in the fire. The college quickly rebounded from the setback. Villagers opened their homes to students. Classes were held in the courthouse. By October of that year, College Hall had been rebuilt—renamed this time for Gov. John W. Davis. (Courtesy Pettaquamscutt Historical Society.)

The building that was to become known as the Alhambra Ballroom was built originally as an exhibition hall in 1903 for the Second Annual New England Association of Arts and Crafts, Inc., Exhibition. The name is seen here painted over the main entrance.

The Auburn Theater Fire, Park Avenue near Elmwood Avenue, 1918. The featured film was *The Rise of Jennie Cushing*, starring the famous silent film star Elsie Ferguson, the day the Auburn Theater was destroyed.

Several members of the Class of 1844 from Providence High School had two interests in common: sailing and seafood. They incorporated as the Squantum Association in 1872 and built the handsome Squantum Club and Clambake Building on the Bay (shown above) in a secluded area off the present Veteran's Memorial Parkway. It had an exclusive membership that was limited to males. It continues its operation today.

A covered carriage moves around a parked cart in this view of Main Street. Could it be headed for the nearby livery stable? (WS)

A serene spot in rural Westerly. (WS)

This photograph of the Larkin Shore House in Watch Hill shows guests enjoying a "one-man band." (WPL)

Peace Dale Library has been the intellectual heart of Peace Dale since the Narragansett Library Association was formed in 1853. The library moved into rooms in what is now the Peace Dale Office Building in 1857 and then to Hazard Memorial Hall upon its construction in 1891. Although much has changed since this vintage 1940s picture, the library—now part of the South Kingstown Public Library system—still provides its patrons with a quiet place for that supreme pleasure, reading. (Courtesy of Peace Dale Library.)

A hurricane-damaged boat at the Warren bridge.

The National Guard was out in force after the Hurricane of 1938. In this photograph, taken from Loafer's Corner, citizens survey damage at the intersection of Hope and State Streets, looking south. The Sparks Block and the YMCA can be clearly seen in the background.

Alfred Vanderbilt's dairy barn with herdsmen, teamsters, and helpers. Oakland's unique dairy barn was bought by railroad financier Robert R. Young. The *Providence Sunday Journal* of November 9, 1947, reported that Young sold all live stock and machinery, and planned to raise sheep.

Old south breaker building, built before 1900. Coal deposits were discovered near Bristol Ferry in 1809; the Rhode Island Coal Company and the Aquidneck Coal Company were soon incorporated and mining began. The coal deposits had been used previous to this, however: British soldiers, in 1760, tried to use the coal for heat, and in 1887 Rhode Island Governor Lippett said that his grandfather had mined Portsmouth coal before 1787. The Portsmouth coal mines were many; there was a mine called the Case Mine (also known as the Aquidneck Mine) at the end of Willow Lane, and one called the New England Mine at the intersection of East Main and Sprague Streets.

Newport Carnival. In August of 1906 a carnival was held to celebrate the arrival of the Atlantic Fleet. This photograph shows decorations at the corner of Mary and Thames Streets.

Whitehall, built in the latter part of the 1800s by Dexter Bradford at the corner of Rhode Island Avenue and Catherine Street. Martin J. Murphy tells the story of the Coogan family who acquired this house in 1903. The family had planned a huge affair for their daughters coming out party. On the night of the party not one guest showed up. It seems that the Coogans were snubbed by Newports 400. It is said that the Coogans walked out of the house that night and returned to Manhattan, never to set foot in Newport again.

At a typical saint day gathering, participants gather to march. This was typical of the feast day attractions that kept the early Italian communities close. The various societies involved provided for social encounters and for the continuance of the worship of hometown patron saints. It was the church that provided almost everything for the newly arrived immigrants. Pastors assisted in finding jobs and homes and in the translation of letters, as the immigrants in many instances could not read or write. The pastors also baptized children, performed marriages, and rendered almost any religious or civil service that an immigrant might need. (Comm. Joseph R. Muratore Collection.)

Pushcart Row is shown here in 1935, when the selling from pushcarts and fruit stands was at its peak and serenity existed—just before the beginning of the Pushcart Struggle. In the upper right-hand corner is the sign of the Federal Hill Pushcart Peddlers Protective Association. During open-air rallies, the windows above the sign were removed and speakers addressed the crowd via a loudspeaker. (Comm. Joseph R. Muratore Collection.)

The Willard Avenue Shopping Area. It was a popular shopping center for the residents of South Providence.

Narragansett Hotel, Providence. Located at the corner of Dorrance and Weybosset Street and completed in 1878, this hotel was purchased in 1924 by Edward Radding and Charles Brown. Max Zinn became a part owner. The hotel had kosher banquet facilities and was the scene of many important events in the Jewish community.

Rocky Point, *c.* 1900. Steamboats were kept busy, especially on Sundays, taking

merrymakers to Rocky Point.

New technology. An early photographer captures a moment in time on Thames Street at Washington Square. (Photograph from the *Daily News*, courtesy of the Newport Historical Society.)

Thames Street. In 1908 Thames Street was paved with belgian blocks—a durable surface that to this day remains in some areas. F.W. Woolworth is on the right.

This aerial photograph, taken in 1972, provides a complete overview of Dutch Island and the remains of Fort Greble. The docking area is visible at the far left. Following down the shore line, the outside walls of the large brick barracks can be observed, and to the right the mining casemate and ordnance storage building can be seen. Just above these is Battery Sedgwick. At the far right are the reservoirs, and to their left are Batteries Mitchell and Hale. A close look at the area below these latter two gun emplacements reveals a number of cellar holes situated in a perfect semi circle, where homes once stood. At the upper end of the photograph, Battery Ogden and the mine commander's position are partially hidden by dense growth. Beyond, on the narrow Lighthouse Reservation, is the site of the granite Civil War battery. Dutch Island Light cannot be seen. (L.H.B. Photograph.)

In the early 1960s Pawtuxet Cove presented a different vista. The building that says "gas" is now a house that belongs to Ray McGarrity. The brick Pawtuxet Athletic Club can be seen at the end of Bridge Street on the right. (William Hall Library Collection.)

Burr's Tavern. Shubael Burr kept a tavern at the southwest corner of Main and Washington (previously King) Streets before the Revolution. Originally a house, Burr turned it into a tavern by adding an extension to the north. In 1775 he became postmaster and the building served as Warren's post office. Letters waiting to be collected were displayed in a front window. Mrs. Burr was among those harassed by Hessian soldiers during the British raid on Warren in 1778. Burr's Tavern hosted many distinguished guests including George Washington (on March 13, 1781), Thomas Jefferson, the Marquis de Lafayette, and Israel Putnam. In his *Travels in North America*, the Marquis de Castellux recorded "I alighted at a good inn the master of which, called Buhr, is remarkable for his size, as well as that of his wife and all his family." After Burr's death in 1790, the building reverted to a dwelling again. When Burr's Tavern was demolished in the early 1900s, local historian Virginia Baker lamented the loss of Warren's ties with an illustrious past.

Crewmen of the *New Hampshire* at drill. Until 1889, the training ship *New Hampshire*, one of the oldest training ships of the American Navy, was stationed at Coasters Harbor Island offshore Newport. It left Newport that year following a severe epidemic among the young men in the training brigades and was replaced by the USS *Constellation* four years later. (Naval War College Museum.)

The 1915 Old Home Day Parade in downtown Pascoag was organized by the Pascoag Fire Department Companies #1 and #2. The large marching contingent is from the Granite Lodge of Pascoag. The street parade went from 9 to 10 am, starting from Fountain Square, Pascoag. A Rhode Island clambake was held at Griffith's Grove from 12 to 3:30 pm, supervised by Mr. Austin of Rocky Point, with at least three tables seating about five hundred people apiece. Speeches by the governor, the lieutenant governor, the congressman, etc. began at 3:30 pm. An aerial exhibition by "Jack" McGee in his Curtis biplane started at 5 pm. A promenade concert and dancing on the grounds, illuminated by electricity as well as by the moonlight from a full moon, occurred on the 26th. Prizes were given to the society making the best appearance, the society having the most members in line, and to the creators of the float or other vehicle making the best appearance.

ORGANIZATIONS

Arcadia would like to thank the following organizations for their contributions to this volume:

American Jewish Historical Society
Blackstone River Valley National Heritage Corridor Commission
Blackstone Valley Historical Society
Bristol Art Exchange
Bristol Phoenix
Charlestown Historical Society
Coalition of Italian American Organizations (CIAO)
Council on America's Military Past
Cranston Historical Society
Cranston Historical Society
East Providence Historical Society
East Providence Planning Department
FourQuest Entertainment
Friends of Linden Place
George Hail Free Library
Heritage Room
Jamestown Historical Society
John D. Rockefeller Library, Brown University
Johnston Historical Society
Kingston Fire District
Kingstown Camera
Little Compton Congregational Church
Manton Hose Co. #1
Massasoit Historical Association
Middletown Police Department
MIT Radiation Laboratory
Mohr Library
Narragansett Chamber of Commerce
Narragansett Fire Department
Narragansett Historical Society
Narragansett Times
National Archives
National Oceanographic and Atmospheric Administration (NOAA)
National Park Service
Naval War College Archives and Museum
Navy Seabee Veterans of America, Island X-1
Newman Congregational Church
Newport Artillery Company
Newport Historical Society
Newport Hospital School of Nursing
Newport Navalog
Newport Restoration Foundation
Nickerson Community Center

Northern Division, Naval Facilities Engineering Command
NUSCOPE
Palisades Mills
Pawtucket Public Library
Pawtucket Red Sox
Pawtucket Times
Pawtuxet Volunteer Fire Co. #1
Peace Dale Fire Department
Peace Dale Library
Pettaquamscutt Historical Society
Phillips Memorial Library
Portsmouth Historical Society
Portsmouth Volunteer Firefighters
Providence College
Providence College Archives
Providence Public Library
Providence Public Library
Prudence Island Historical and Preservation Society
Quonset Air Museum
Records Service
Rhode Island Economic Development Corporation
Rhode Island Historical Preservation Commission
Rhode Island Jewish Historical Association
Rhode Island Public Transit Authority
Robert Beverly Hale Library
Roger Williams University, Public Relations Office
Rose Island Lighthouse Foundation
Slater Mill Historic Site
Society for the Preservation of New England Antiquities
South County Hospital
South County Museum
South County Museum
South Kingstown Library
South Kingstown Police Department
Spaulding Research House
Sprague Mansion
St. Ann's Church
St. Bartholomew Church
St. Mary Society
St. Mary's Church
St. Mary's Episcopal Church
Town of Lincoln
Town of Narragansett
Trinity Church
United States Army Military History Institute
United States Coast Guard
United States Marine Corps
United States Naval Academy
United States Naval Institute
United States Navy
United States Navy Historical Center
University of Rhode Island Graduate School of Oceanography
University of Rhode Island Library, Special Collections
University of Rhode Island, Special Collections
Visiting Nurse Service
Warwick Historical Society
Westerly Historical Society
Westerly Public Library
Westerly Sun
What Cheer Postcard Club
William Hall Library